MW01624292

The Power of the Undisturbed Mind

Austin Gordon, Ph.D

First printing 2000

Cover design by Kurma Rupa Dasa
Interior design by Chaitanya Chandra Dasa
Printed in India
Published simultaneously in the United States of America and Canada by Torchlight Publishing, Inc.

Library of Congress Cataloging-in-Publication Data

Gordon, Austin, 1950-
Eye of the storm : The power of the undisturbed mind / Gordon Austin
p. cm.
Includes biographical references.
ISBN: 1-887089-24-1
1.Peace of mind—Religious aspects—Hinduism. 2. Spiritual life—Hinduism. 3.Awareness. I. Title.

BL1215.P4 G67 2000
294.5'44—dc21 00-037729

For more information, contact the Publisher:

Torchlight Publishing
PO Box 52, Badger, CA 93603
Telephone: (559) 337-2200, Fax: (559) 337-2354
Email: torchlight@spiralcomm.net Web: www.torchlight.com

CONTENTS

Introduction

The mind can be our friend or our enemy. When disturbed, it is the repository of anxiety, anger, and materialistic attachment – three forces that disrupt our natural tranquility and clarity of thought. When undisturbed by these agents, however, the mind becomes our unswerving friend, acting as a powerful tool to help invoke our innate spiritual awareness. But how to turn our minds from enemy to friend, especially in the frantically paced and data-overloaded age we live in? Fortunately, genuine spiritual knowledge remains unaffected by the veneer of modernity, and so, in spite of the nature of our times, we are still able to benefit fully from the wisdom contained in the world's great cultural traditions. These timeless teachings, which form the basis of

The Eye of the Storm, offer invaluable guidance in freeing ourselves of the anxieties and misconceptions that cover our natural serenity and blissfulness.

With the advancement of communication and transportation technologies, interaction between cultures has reached unprecedented levels. As a result, societies throughout the world have generally become more open-minded and informed about one another. In recent years, for example, healing practices from the world's older civilizations have become increasingly popular, with herbal remedies and techniques such as acupuncture being appreciated as simple and natural, yet often highly effective, means to promote healing.

The time-tested cultures of our world also offer great insight into the art of developing a mind free from unwanted disturbances. Although when read in their original form these teachings may appear somewhat alien or esoteric to contemporary readers, the principles they embody are as relevant today as when originally composed. *The Eye of the Storm: The Power of the Undisturbed Mind* presents a concise, easy-to-read synthesis of these perspectives and practices, which, although ancient, give us all necessary information for achieving sublime consciousness.

To facilitate our understanding of the central concepts of *The Eye of the Storm*, Chapter One gives a complete account of the traditional Eastern view of the human mind. The reader, perhaps due to cultural influences, may wish to accept as metaphorical such descriptions of the mind as part of the subtle body. Fortunately, such a non-literal view presents no obstacle to the utility of the ideas, for they are perfectly suited to being employed as heuristics, or learning devices. At the same time, the ideas do in fact form a cogent alternative to modern views on the nature of the mind and the self, and therefore we also welcome the reader to consider them in this light. In fact, there is a growing body of scientific research that offers support for the traditional ideas presented here. In either case, the representations are ideally suited for the present purpose, which is to further our understanding of our inner selves and aid our progress toward our natural, peaceful psychological condition.

Chapters Two, Three, and Four address the three primary forces of mental disquiet, namely, material attachment, fear, and anger. In each of these chapters the nature of the particular disruptive agent is carefully analyzed, as well as what measures we can take to reduce its pernicious influence. The book concludes with Chapter Five, which turns to a discussion of the three qualities that pervade our mind's interaction with the world. Known in Sanskrit as *gunas*, these primary modes act dynamically to influence our every thought and action, and Chapter Five presents this ancient and fascinating perspective in a "user-friendly" manner.

Real enjoyment, as opposed to ephemeral pleasure, requires equipoise and insight into the true nature of things. Or, as the *Bhagavad-gita* explains, without peace there can be no happiness. By pursuing our spiritual growth with intelligence and sincerity, we will come to increasingly experience life without the burden of unnecessary anxiety, anger, and material attachment, and by so doing, we will develop the serenity and self-awareness that is our birthright.

Chapter One

The Mind and the Subtle Body

Although we live with them every day, our minds remain mysterious. Reflecting a not uncommon attitude, contemporary philosopher A. J. Ayer refused to study the mind because "it has no locus;" in other words, he is uncertain where or what it is. Current scientific research into the nature of the mind generally assumes that our minds somehow "emerge" from the physical brain and its various states. This is all vague and speculative, however, for brain states are nothing more than complex patterns arising from the interaction of billions of neurons. Nevertheless, according to adherents to this view, the mind is merely a by-product of the brain's atomic structure, which is completely describable by physical laws in terms of mass, charge, spin, etc. Most of us recoil at this starkly impersonal and materialistic depiction of our thoughts and feelings, finding it counterintuitive and foreign to the deep emotions and powerful sense of personal identity we experience. However, for the hard-core proponents of this explanation, such objections are dismissed as misguided sentiment, born from our fantasies and longings, and therefore without foundation in reality. Some predict that eventually all such sentimentality will be set aside, and the day will come when, in the words of molecular biologist James Watson, all aspects of our being will "...be completely understood in terms of the coordinative interactions of small and large molecules."

No one questions the idea that the brain and the mind are closely related. Changes in brain states, such as those induced by ingesting drugs or alcohol, create pronounced effects on our mental condition. However, the precise nature of this relation still remains open to discussion. "All that the observed scientific facts suggest is that there is a close correlation between mental events and cerebral events," explains S. Chennakesavhan. "But this regular synchronism may well suggest, not that they are identical, but that there is a higher unity whose behests are being obeyed."

Historically, some notable Western philosophers have argued that the conscious self is independent of the physical body. For example, Rene Descartes' first philosophical premise was that our capacity for thought is incontrovertible evidence of our personal existence. His famous statement, "I think, therefore I am," is the cornerstone of this view, which distinguishes the self from matter (the body) by its ability to think and sense. Spinoza also saw the conscious self as an entirely different "substance" than matter, and Kant recognized that every thought belongs to an individual who has a direct and unified awareness of the thought.

These ideas parallel the traditional Eastern perspective, which sees consciousness as distinct from and independent of the body. In this view, consciousness and personality are fundamental features of reality; they do not emerge from neural activity in the physical brain. Although it is via our consciousness that we know material objects and events, we cannot know consciousness itself through our senses or their extensions as material instruments, because of its non-physical nature. Consciousness can, of course, be directly experienced; the reality of our own conscious perceptions is certainly undeniable. As renowned scientist John

Eccles writes in *The Human Mind,* "My approach to conscious experience is, in the first instance, based on my direct experience of my own self-consciousness." This simple but critical point is also made by physicist Eugene Wigner, who explains that quantum theory is deficient in its failure to account for consciousness, for consciousness "is primary and the basis of our knowledge of all other things."

Although the terms "mind" and "consciousness" are often used interchangeably by Western psychologists, as we turn to traditional Eastern psychology we find the two are clearly distinguished. In the Eastern view, the mind is not itself conscious but is understood to be a subtle material mechanism connecting the physical body (including the brain) to the conscious self. It is not part of the visible physical body but is part of the subtle aspect of our being (or subtle body), and is composed of matter so fine that our physical senses cannot directly perceive it. Unlike denser material elements, which we can touch or taste, the subtle body is known only by inference and self-examination.

The concept of subtle matter is generally unfamiliar to people who have not studied Eastern metaphysics, but in those traditions it is central to the study and practice of psychology and spirituality. Although a detailed explanation would carry us away from our topic, it is important to at least understand that in its finer states, matter is no less real than when it is "gross" or tangible; in fact, it is actually more powerful and enduring. In relation to the mind, its formation from subtle energy removes some of the limitations imposed by the natural laws governing energy of greater density. As the physical elements such as earth, water, fire, and air each possess different properties and capacities, so the subtle energy of the mind possesses unique characteristics. These capabilities include the capacity to liaison between the conscious self and the physical world, much as computer software interfaces between the computer user and the system's hardware. In other words, the mind, along with the intelligence, allows the conscious self to interact with the physical body and the general environment.

The conscious self is therefore housed in two bodies, one physical and one subtle. The physical body is readily apparent to all our senses, while the subtle body, composed of mind and intelligence, may be known only by its symptoms. For example, when we hear a person explain something in a logical manner – as opposed to rambling on incoherently—we understand that we are interacting with that person's intelligence. Or, if we see someone respond to various sensory inputs in an organized and functional way—as opposed to behaving in a paranoid or schizophrenic manner—we recognize that we are witnessing a properly working mind. Moods and attitudes are also manifestations of the subtle mental energy. Of course, we can also directly experience the activities of our own subtle body, as our minds integrate sense perceptions and our intelligence guides our choices and activities.

In the Sanskrit language the mind is called a *yantra,* or mechanical instrument. As an invariable companion of the self, it is subtle matter, material and unconscious, which assists the self in gaining knowledge. The senses, centered about the mind, are channels through which the mind apprehends objects within the physical world. An analogy helpful for understanding the relation of the self to the gross and subtle body is that of a five-horse chariot, the chariot driver, and the reins. In this depiction, the physical body is compared to the chariot, pulled forward by five horses, representing the five senses. The chariot driver (the intelligence) guides the five horses (the senses). The chariot driver (intelligence) controls the horses (senses) by reins, which represent the mind. Therefore, through the instrument of the mind, the intelligence guides and regulates sense activity. The conscious self rides as a passenger in the chariot, relying on the intelligence and the mind to steer it toward its intended destination. However, if the driver (intelligence) becomes weak or confused, the powerful horses (the senses) can tear the reins (the mind) from his hands. At this point, the guiding instrument becomes simply a tool for the fickle reactions of unchecked horses, which can be compared to the mind overwhelmed by sense desire.

The mind is the coordinating instrument that connects the intelligence (the driver) to the bodily senses (the horses), and all three (senses, mind, and intelligence) assist the self in learning about the world around us. As the chariot example illustrates, the *self* is not an instrument, but it is the personal subject—the one who experiences. It is the "I" whom we indicate when we say, "I see" or "I feel." Because the mind is a tool in the hands of the intelligence, it is the intelligence with its power of discrimination that determines what the mind will accept (*sankalpa*) and what it will reject (*vikalpa*). This process is nothing more than what we commonly refer to as "making up our minds," where the mind suspends action while the intelligence analyzes the alternatives.

In the ancient spiritual text *Srimad Bhagavatam,* we also find an intriguing allegory pertaining to the relation between the gross body, the subtle body, and the self. The central character in this story, King Puranjana, represents a person searching the world for enjoyment. King Puranjana, symbolizing the self, enters the City of Nine Gates— a metaphor for the physical body and its nine openings (eyes, nose, ears, etc.) In this beautiful city, Puranjana meets a lovely woman (representing intelligence) whom he marries and makes his queen. Just as we use our intelligence to make arrangements for our comfort and pleasure, with the help of his queen (the intelligence), the king enjoys life in the City of Nine Gates (the physical body).

The story of King Puranjana illustrates how the mind coordinates the activities of the senses, interfaces between the conscious self and the various sensations, and brings information to the intelligence (the queen) for consideration. The queen (the intelligence) directs the attention of King Puranjana (the self) to this world and its display of light, sound, taste, etc., which he mistakes for the complete reality.

To explain this ancient allegory in contemporary terms, the mind is compared to multimedia computer software capable of integrating audio and visual materials into a single display of sense data. A scientist commenting on the allegory of Puranjana wrote, "Employing a computer analogy, we might say Puranjana represents the user, the City of Nine Gates the computer hardware, and the queen the software that allows the user to interface with the hardware and use it for practical purposes.... The whole system resembles a computer-generated virtual reality."

The mind's central role in sense perception is also evident when we consider the many occasions when, although we are receiving sense stimulation (such as hearing music), our attention is elsewhere. In these instances it can be said that we are really unaware, or unmindful, of the stimulation. This can even occur visually, as when "lost in thought" while walking or – hopefully not too often – while driving a vehicle. A poem from the *Upanishads* captures this idea: "My mind was elsewhere, I did not see. My mind was elsewhere, I did not hear. It is with the mind truly that one sees. It is with the mind that one hears." Because the mind presents sensations to the conscious self, things are not really "sensed" unless the mind attends to them.

According to this view, even the experience of being aware of more than one thing at a time is a misconception. This sense of simultaneity is actually due to the mind's rapid transition from one perception to another.

Working in conjunction with our intelligence, the mind continually accepts or rejects (*sankalpa* and *vikalpa*) whatever it encounters. A vivid present-day example of this is "channel surfing," where we view a program for a short time, then reject it in favor of another. This rapid-fire process may appear to be automatic, as the mind quickly scans a selection and then accepts or rejects. But even in this case, the intelligence is judging the sensory input based on certain criteria it has established as important, and the mind behaves in a manner comparable to being programmed. For example, a young man may carefully consider television shows full of intense action and strong visual stimulation, while immediately rejecting the soap opera genre out of hand. This is due to the intelligence "writing a program" for the mind upon which it bases its active function of accepting or rejecting. Every experience involves some act of will, and this will is due to the intelligence, which resolves how the individual should respond.

The mind's subtle operation can also be

understood by considering how it integrates our sensations of taste, smell, etc., and provides us with a unified picture of the world even though the sensations themselves are separate. For example, brain research has revealed how human vision involves three anatomically and functionally distinct systems: one for shape, one for color, and one for motion. Scientists have no clear idea of how the three systems are combined to produce the fully integrated vision we actually experience, but according to Eastern thought it is the subtle mind, operating on higher-order principles, that accomplishes this mysterious task. In a similar way, our consciousness of the world is continuous; we experience no gaps or jumps as each moment is seamlessly woven into the next. This continuity of awareness is indispensable to a meaningful reality, but it would be impossible if the mind were made up of merely sensations and brain. Sensations are essentially nerve impulses and, as such, are not aware of anything. They are comparable to the patterns of electrons that form and disappear in a computer's circuitry as it produces images. Bertrand Russell explains this relation: "Sensations may be defined as the intersection of mind and matter….They are not themselves knowledge, but they supply the data for our knowledge of the physical world." Therefore, it is the subtle mind that organizes the sense data and presents them to the personal consciousness, where we find meaning in experience.

Some final evidence supporting the traditional Eastern concept of the mind can be drawn from research into paranormal psychology. Some are understandably skeptical of paranormal psychological research, for by its very nature it has greater potential for abuse and fabrication than typical research efforts. Many times, however, opposition is not based on specific objections to experimental protocols but is merely a "gut reaction" to the entire field. This attitude is embodied in the comment of a reviewer for a scientific journal article on the paranormal, who wrote, "This is the kind of thing I would not believe even if it existed."

Fortunately, many other scientists adopt a more open-minded stance. For example, after producing a documentary on paranormal psychological research for Thames Television, a well-known British biologist concluded, "A scientist would have to be either massively ignorant or a confirmed bigot to deny the evidence that the human mind can make connection with space, time, and matter in ways which have nothing to do with the ordinary senses. Further, he cannot deny that these connections are compatible with current thinking in physics, and may in the future become accepted as a part of an extended science."

Paranormal psychology embraces a number of areas: Precognition (foreknowledge); telepathy (communication from one mind to another at a distance other than through the main senses); clairvoyance (faculty of seeing mentally what is happening or what exists out of sight); and psychokinesis (the movement of physical objects by mental influence without physical contact). Also, research into out-of-body experiences and reincarnation memories are generally considered part of the field of paranormal psychology. Many carefully conducted scientific research endeavors, some of which have been carried out at leading universities (for example, Robert Jahn at Princeton, Carl Sargent at Cambridge University, physicists Targ and Putoff at Stanford, etc.) offer empirical support for the mind's ability to cross time and distance, to see things out of sight, and to directly affect matter. Overall, "[Their] results suggest that information can directly cross space between minds...and that information may turn out to be the basic commodity in the universe." The mental capabilities documented in paranormal psychological research have no explanation within the confines of the theoretical view that the mind is a by-product of the brain. However, the traditional Eastern conception of the mind as part of a subtle body composed of ultra-fine matter— matter that is not restricted by the same physical laws that govern it in its grosser manifestations—provides an explanatory basis for these seemingly mysterious events.

Another example of direct evidence for a subtle but material mind is the well-known occurrence of distinct sensations, such as twinges of pain or itching, by persons whose arms or legs have been amputated. This is generally referred to as the experience of "phantom limbs." Since the mind is subtle matter, it is conceivable that it could act on gross matter without going through the related physical sense organ, a fact that could also explain the many reports of out-of-body or near death experiences. In these events, the body is incapacitated due to anesthesia or shock, while the mind apparently separates itself and remains completely conscious and lucid. In cases occurring in hospital operating rooms, patients have recalled precise details of the specific procedures they were undergoing, in contrast to typical patients who (as one would expect) have no recollection and can offer only the most generalized descriptions of what their procedure may have entailed.

In this chapter we've briefly presented the traditional Eastern view of the human mind and its relation to the physical body and the conscious self. Although deriving from cultures and teachings that are thousands of years old, the Eastern concept of the mind as a subtle material mechanism still stands as a viable model of the human psyche. In fact, in many important ways it offers a more complete and natural explanation of the mind-body connection than do theories currently in vogue. But as discussed earlier, the ideas and practices suggested in the following chapters do not require one to literally accept this view of the nature of the mind. The subtle mind concept is also valuable simply as a tool for helping to effectively communicate the many practical ideas that follow.

The mind can be either the friend or enemy of the self; this idea is central to each of the perspectives that we will discuss. Acting as a friend, it works under the guidance of a strong and positive intelligence to further our self-improvement and personal growth. But, just as an infection can overcome the efficacy of a medicine, so the mind, by overcoming intelligence and the higher principles it should hold, becomes our enemy. In doing so, it pulls our thoughts and feelings away from our ideals, potentially deteriorating our standards of right and wrong. "One who cannot control the mind lives with the greatest enemy," says the *Bhagavad-gita*. It is as if one gives power-of-attorney to an incompetent or untrustworthy person, who then loses one's inheritance. Because our interaction with the world occurs through the agency of the mind, when undisciplined it wastes our potential for spiritual insight.

Undoubtedly the mind possesses great strength that can be used for our benefit, but this same power can be transformed into a misguided obstinacy that holds fast to negative patterns of thought and behavior. These patterns then become further ingrained by repetition. For example, consider the miserable condition of life created by extreme obsessive-compulsive behavior, where the mind rules over the person's life like a cruel tyrant, demanding obedience to every whim no matter how impractical or humiliating.

When the mind acts as an enemy, it engages three principal accomplices in its work. In broad terms, these are known as anger, fear, and attachment. But although these influences are forceful, they can be managed and overcome through practice. They are effective only when, due to our weakened spiritual condition, we empower them. By bringing the mind more sharply under our control, we can use its tenacity and energy to help drive out these three disturbing influences and move toward our natural inner peace.

How to do so is the subject of the following chapters, which offer some carefully selected perspectives from the great spiritual traditions of the East. It is our firm conviction that by incorporating these simple, time-tested approaches, we take an invaluable step toward attaining the all-important goal of an undisturbed mind.

Chapter Two

Attachment and Detachment

Attachment is one of the three principle forces that disturb the human mind. To better understand how this is true, we need to explore the sense in which the word "attachment" is used in Eastern thought. In the Eastern context, attachment is distinguished from affection, which refers to the natural emotional connection we feel for other living beings. Such wholesome feelings are not to be shunned or repressed, for they help us become more compassionate and tolerant. As we grow emotionally, intellectually, and spiritually, our sense of affection for others is not lost; rather, it is refined and expanded.

Attachment, on the other hand, refers to a self-centered dependence on material objects and mundane relations. It involves a turning of our minds toward materialism and a materialistic sense of the self, and under the influence of strong attachment, we therefore become dependent on the "external" for enjoyment. When attachment covers the mind, our attention is focused on material acquisitions and bodily gratification, and we fail to appreciate the deeper spiritual reality that surrounds us. Neglecting our higher, freer nature, we deprive ourselves of the sublime experience of enlightened consciousness.

From the spiritual texts of the East we learn that we must cultivate detachment as an "antidote" to excessive attachment. Sometimes the concept of detachment is misunderstood and may conjure up images of broken relationships, separation from things dear, or even a cold, uncaring aloofness. This is a distorted sense of the idea, however, for in fact detachment is a necessary and positive force that balances our minds and is crucial to our psychological and spiritual well-being. Detachment brings great strength to our lives, allowing us to step away from people, events, or behaviors that have become deleterious. For this reason, Eastern teachings compare detachment to the "surgeon's scalpel," illustrating how it empowers us to "cut away" things that are harmful to our self-development.

Because we are by nature pleasure-seeking,

sometimes the idea of detachment is seen as a threat to our enjoying propensity. But this is also a false notion, for while human beings certainly desire pleasure, we recognize that everything has a cost, and to gain one thing we often must give up something else. Marriage has advantages, but it also means sacrificing independence and accepting many material responsibilities. Following a vegetarian diet means no more "Big Macs," but we gain important health and ethical benefits. In the same way, some measure of sense control and renunciation is necessary if we wish to taste the serenity of higher spiritual awareness.

For this reason, learning to control our urges for immediate gratification has long been an integral part of the educational process. (Unfortunately, today's higher education is mostly concerned with the development of technical and commercial skills—a fact many people see as contributing to our current moral and ethical crises.) Every functioning society understands this and therefore encourages its members to cultivate at least a measure of detachment.

Our religious traditions are, of course, tightly interwoven with our educational values and contribute much to our understanding in this area. These traditions remind us that our enthusiasm to enjoy can easily become excessive and lead to irresponsibility, errors in judgement, and general unhappiness. In Sanskrit, this tendency to indulge our senses is called *maya,* or forgetfulness of our spiritual selves. But the spirit of detachment wards off this *maya,* as it cools our passions and permits us to regain our equilibrium, our "center." The *Bhagavad-Gita* emphasizes the importance of detachment by explaining the temporary nature of all our desires. "The nonpermanent appearance of happiness and distress, and their disappearance in due course, are like the appearance and disappearance of winter and summer seasons. They arise from sense perception, and one must learn to tolerate them without being disturbed." The great renunciate Lord Buddha also explained to his followers, "Craving leads to suffering, and ignorance perpetuates our craving." The ignorance he spoke of is "ignoring" the actual nature of this world, that is, imagining it to be the place "where we belong." Because we are spiritual beings, the material world is inherently incompatible with the actual needs of the higher self. Knowing this to be true is called *sambandha,* or awareness of our spiritual essence.

Therefore, the quality of renunciation is necessary for a life of mental contentment and self-understanding. The nature of the disturbed mind is to hover, then dart in pursuit of one desire after another. But chasing these flickering desires brings neither peace nor happiness. First of all, even if we acquire a material object that we have desired, be it a new watch, a favorite car, or whatever, that object has a limited capacity to satisfy us. It may fulfill a particular craving, but because each of our desires represents only a tiny fraction of our complete self, even completely satisfying that one desire will leave us largely unfulfilled. Second, and more importantly, the things of this world are material, but we are spiritual beings. Therefore, the self can only vicariously experience material enjoyments. Because of this inherent alienation between the spiritual self and material gratification, the fleeting sensations of bodily enjoyment cannot satisfy our deeper needs. For this reason we are constantly turning our attention to things new and different, only to again repeat the same cycle.

Often we find our daily lives so demanding and time-consuming that we "ignore" our true selves and become caught up in thoughts of "I, me, and mine." We imagine "*I* am Mr. So and So, these people work for *me*, this is *my* house, and this bank balance is *mine*," with little regard for *sambandha*, or awareness of our identity beyond this temporary body. Unfortunately, most of the dominant forces in our modern societies contribute to our materialistic tendencies and actively promote the view that we are consumers and enjoyers of our physical bodies. In such a consumer-oriented environment, it is especially important to consciously cultivate detachment as a safeguard against this false conception of who we are. The endeavor to accumulate possessions has the potential to dominate our lives. But because our time is so fleeting, we should be careful not to over-invest our time and emotions in the struggle for material gain.

When unchecked by detachment, materialistic attitudes inevitably spill over into our personal relations. If our own bodily identification is too strong, we fail to see the sacredness of others; instead, they are viewed in terms of their "usefulness" to our own purposes. Here again the contrast between affection and attachment is put into focus. A mood of service and an absence of the need to control characterize affection, which is a partial manifestation of our spiritual loving propensity. Conversely, attachment causes us to objectify and depersonalize others. Because attachment grows out of the needs of our false ego (or the sense of identity conditioned by materialism), it transforms into bitterness or anger when threatened with separation or loss. The attached person becomes frustrated when deprived of the craved interaction and looks to blame the resulting despondency on some outside agent, often the former object of attachment. In this way love and attachment are like day and night. The former is positive, making us openhearted, and can potentially expand into unconditional spiritual love. The latter is rooted in our frailties and insecurities; it creates a prison for the soul by keeping the mind focused on the mundane and the petty.

Directly or indirectly, most of us have experienced personal relationships involving excessive attachment. Since we admire strength in others, such dependency or "neediness" diminishes the appeal of the relationship. Perceiving a measure of detachment in the other is a balancing force that reassures us of the other's inner security and spiritual depth.

Time and Change

From the vast expanses of space to the micro-universe of the atom, the world around us is ever-changing. In the face of such inconstancy, we attempt to get a "fix" on reality by classifying and categorizing the things we find around us. The well-known German philosopher Nietzsche made this observation, explaining that we impose labels and place people and objects into groups in an attempt to give a stability and certainty to a world that is, in fact, in a constant state of flux. We need and want objects in the world to have an identity that persists over time, so we create a "necessary fiction" (what he called a "regularity of perceptions") to allow us to feel secure.

The struggle for this "regularity of perception" is especially pronounced in cultures oriented toward the modern scientific worldview, and therefore the perspectives of traditional societies offer a contrast to this tendency to impose order on a world in flux. For example, while most of us seemingly live by the clock and all variety of timetables, the language of the Hopi Indians contains no words, grammatical forms, or expressions that refer directly to what we call "time." Neither do the Hopi Indians speak in terms of past, present, or future, either explicitly or implicitly. This may seem strange to people educated in the Euclidean and Newtonian tradition, who are accustomed to perceiving the world as the interaction of homogeneous three-dimensional space and the flowing of time. But it is perfectly valid to have descriptions of the world around us that do not contrast space and time. In fact, Einstein's relativity, which is the accepted view of modern physics, is one such alternative view—one conceived in mathematical terms. Similarly, the Hopi view is another—one we may see as composed in a language of mystical quality.

In the same vein, the concepts of material impermanence and spiritual permanence are deeply interwoven into the Wintu tribes' worldview. Their religious teachings emphasize how all material forms are transient and fleeting, and the principal characters in their religious stories (the Coyote, the Grizzly Bear, the Buzzard) never assume stable forms. As the Wintus explain, their view of the natural world as always changing stands in relation to their awareness of the immutability of the spiritual essence.

Asian philosophical thought also embraces this understanding of the fluid nature of the world around us, informing us that objects we encounter do not really "persist" in the way we normally imagine them to. Author Alan Watts nicely captures the essence of the Eastern perspective when he writes, "A living body is not a fixed thing but a flowing event, like a flame or a whirlpool. The shape alone is stable, for the substance is a stream of energy going in one end and out the other."

Although the Eastern view of how things transform over time may seem unfamiliar to us, it is actually more common sense than the rather fuzzy ideas about change that we ordinarily carry around with us. To help see this, let's carefully consider what is occurring when we look at an object over a period of time. In our everyday thinking, when we observe something, we assume that we are receiving the visual image of a stable object, i.e., a "single thing" that is persisting over time. For example, if we watch the flame of a candle for five minutes, we think we have been looking at the flame. However, upon more careful reflection, we understand that we've actually been witnessing the rapid replacement of one flame-state by another. Again, "The shape alone is stable, for the substance is a stream of energy going in one end and out the other."

The traditional teachings of the East are in accord with this explanation, saying that what we perceive as a "single persisting object" (e.g., a flame or a flower) is in reality a series of similar, but nevertheless discrete, objects. So a flower bud does not change or transform into a full-bloomed flower; instead, a new flower, representing the next stage in its development, is presented to us at each moment.

Obviously, this deconstruction of everyday objects into final, immutable, and wholly discrete moments completely overturns the notion of change as we commonly understand it. But there is an undeniable logic to this admittedly unfamiliar view. The 19th century philosopher Francis Herbert Bradley pointed to this when he reasoned, "If something endures without any change for even the tiniest imaginable amount of time, then by simple logic it must endure forever."

To illustrate his point, he asks us to visualize something (such as a flower) changing from one state to another. At moment **A** it is in state **A**, and at moment **B** it is in state **B** (we might say it has grown, or blossomed, the tiniest bit). But in order to visualize this, we apparently have two choices. One, the flower "jumps" or "quantum leaps" from state **A** to state **B** as the new moment arises. This is essentially the Eastern view described above, where our perception of change is comparable to the experience of watching a motion picture. In a motion picture, individual snapshots are run together at a speed that creates the appearance of change (or motion), when in fact there is only a series of discrete frames.

The second, more familiar view is that objects smoothly transform from one state to another. There is no "jumping" because state **A** and state **B** are connected by an unlimited series of "sub-steps." Ironically, when closely analyzed, this more familiar explanation begins to resemble something out of Alice in Wonderland, *because it never actually confronts the fact that things do change*. By not allowing objects to "jump" from one state to the next, it must constantly appeal to the next level of change, each tinier than the preceding one. Since this regress would go on infinitely, an actual point of change is never reached. So although appearing simple and straightforward, our ordinary view actually eliminates change, leaving us only with an infinite regression. We can never move forward, so we never get anywhere! Clearly, when this idea of change is scrutinized, it appears less simple than we might suppose.

Because change is a condition of never being the same, it is inherently mysterious to the human mind. In the Sanskrit language, the material world is called "*asat*," or "non-existent," and the *Bhagavad-gita* speaks of its elusive quality: "Those who are seers of the truth have concluded that of the non-existent there is no endurance and of the existent there is no cessation. This they have concluded by studying the nature of both." Thus, the Gita confirms the religious stories of the Wintu, which remind us that the material energy is relentless mutable, while spirit is eternal.

In his book *Wholeness and the Implicate Order*, David Bohm, Professor of Physics at the University of London, offers some fascinating descriptions of how matter changes form. He approaches physics from a holistic rather than a reductionist perspective, that is, rather than attempting to understand reality by dissecting it into smaller and smaller parts, he starts with the assumption that the universe is unified, and therefore, science must take that underlying unity into account.

Bohm's ideas are relevant to our topic because they are helpful in showing how some of the findings of modern physics support the Vedic description of how material objects actually change. Bohm writes of an "implicate" (or enfolded) universe and an "explicate" (unfolded) universe, explaining that matter is constantly popping up into the explicate order from the implicate order. This exchange creates a perpetual "cosmic dance" between the manifest and unmanifest, or between an actual electron-like "existence" and "non-existence." Importantly, his description is not a creative fancy but adheres to the rigorous mathematical standards of his field. At the same time, it also resolves many of the problems that have stymied more traditional explanations.

To assist our understanding of the concept of implicate and explicate orders, Bohm offers the following experiment. He takes a cylindrical jar filled with glycerin and affixes a rod through the center to rotate the jar. A drop of black ink is then placed on the surface of the glycerin. Because the glycerin is thick, the drop sits on the surface. When the jar is rotated, the ink drop draws out into a thinner and thinner line, until it eventually disappears. This disappearance corresponds to the enfolding of matter into the implicate order. Then the turning of the rod is reversed, and gradually the ink reappears, first as a thin line and then as the original drop. Similarly, although material objects appear to be stable and stationary, they are, in reality, flickering projections. However, due to our limited perceptual abilities, we perceive them as enduring images. In language that closely parallels the Vedic description, Bohm explains that the manifestation of matter is rather like motion picture film passing through the projector.

The Vedas continue to explain that because our physical bodies are objects in the material world, they are also transforming at every moment, growing from infancy to childhood, then to youth, middle, and finally old age. The renowned Vedic scholar A.C. Bhaktivedanta Swami describes the journey of the self through these different physical forms as "changing bodies." "We are not *growing*, but we are *changing bodies*," he explains. Continuing his description, he compares *growth* to a moving figure in a film, where the "movement" is actually the combination of many pictures. According to the Vedas, the conscious (non-material) self is continually accepting new bodies, one after another. "Therefore the child is speaking one way, but when he is older he speaks differently, because he has accepted a different body."

The transcendent self, as pure consciousness, is beyond time and space and therefore does not change, i.e., it is eternal. Even in this life we see that while our bodies move from youth to old age, each of us remains, as the self within, essentially the same person. Our attitudes may mature, but the inner person, our most authentic self, remains intact. The events of our past, for example, were most certainly our personal experiences, not those of some other person simply "linked" to us. According to Eastern spiritual teachings, the conscious self endures the death of the body and takes another birth to continue its spiritual quest. This is described in the *Gita*: "As a person puts on new garments, giving up old ones, the soul similarly accepts new material bodies, giving up the old and useless ones."

Death And Dying

Whether we cultivate a sense of detachment during our lives or not, all our attachments will be sundered at the time of our leaving this world. Schopenhauer said that contemplation of death was the beginning of philosophy, and Montaigne once wrote that "to philosophize is to learn to die."

Although "for he who has taken birth, death is certain," we often avoid serious thoughts about our personal mortality, or, for that matter, the demise of loved ones. According to psychologists who have studied the various attitudes people hold toward death, this avoidance is in large part due to underlying feelings of fear or dread. They explain that while people today attempt to appear more indifferent to their own passing, internally they are more anxious than ever before. One author writes, "The old religious assurances that there would be a gathering-in someday have been largely discarded and [replaced by] neuroses caused by fear." Harvard theologian Krister Stendhal agrees, explaining that while many moderns try to mimic Socrates' "good cheer and comfort" as he approached death, their actual mood is one of "desertion and loneliness."

Not surprisingly, a principal cause of fear for many people is the notion that death means they will cease to exist. Although such a state of "non-being" is not properly imaginable, thinking that someday there will be no more *me* can understandably induce a sense of discomfort. Some assert that personal non-being threatens them not, such as the acclaimed philosopher Ludwig Wittgenstein, who said, "Death is not an event in life, because death is not lived through." The same attitude is put forward by the ancient Greek Epicurus, who claimed, "When I am, death is not. When death is, I am not. Therefore, I can never have anything to do with death." Obviously, such views consider the self to be nothing more than a by-product of the material body and reject any conception of a non-material self, or soul. Bertrand Russell expressed such disbelief in any eternal self when he wrote, "Blind and powerless is man's life; on him and all his race the slow, sure death falls pitiless and dark. Blind to good and evil, reckless of destruction, omnipotent matter rolls on its relentless way."

However, most people find the notion of a meaningless void after death intolerable and illogical, and they conceive of an enduring spiritual existence after the demise of the physical body. For them, the essence of our personality, our "soul" or "spirit," is understood as non-material and not subject to the influence of time. As the *Gita* states, "For the soul there is neither birth nor death at any time. He has not come into being, does not come into being, and will not come into being. He is unborn, eternal, ever-existing, and primeval. He is not slain when the body is slain." The *Tao Te Ching* also speaks of the enduring nature of the spirit: "See all things however they flourish, they return to the root from which is called Quietness. One who possesses it, though his body ceases, he is not destroyed." Or as Socrates declared confidently on the eve of his death, "You will bury only my body, not me."

The *Vedas* liken our passing from this world to an examination, wherein the consciousness and qualities we have developed throughout our lives are "put to the test." When we are forced to exit our material bodies, it is critical that we not be overly attached to the temporary connections binding us to this world. Accordingly, the *Vedas* enjoin us to educate ourselves in the higher reality of our spiritual identities. Without this understanding, the mind is traumatized by the experience of leaving behind all that we imagine to be "ourselves." In such a condition, dread, fear, and sorrow will overwhelm us, and we will miss the opportunity to be transferred to the highest destination by remembering God.

At the time of death we confront ourselves as we really are; there remains no place for the self-delusions or rationalizations we may have used to "smooth over" our reprehensible behavior. The naked truth of who we are and what we hold dear is laid before our eyes, without the protective embellishments our egos have always been quick to provide. It is, indeed, the ultimate "reality check." If we have developed no detachment and only pursued worldly enjoyments, we will be ill prepared for the swift separation imposed by death. But if we have come to know ourselves as non-material persons belonging to the spiritual world, our passing will be a joyous release from the bondage of birth and death. As the poet Gibran has written, "And what is it to cease breathing but to free the breath from its restless tides, that it may rise and expand and seek God unencumbered."

Chapter Three

Without Anxiety

Fear disquiets us. As a survival instinct it alerts us to danger, preparing us to respond swiftly to hazardous situations, such as a driver swerving into our lane or the loss of our footing on a stairway. Fear arises from psychological as well as physical threats, such as concerns over social status, visual appearance, or professional competency. Being without confidence in our abilities is an obvious cause of such mental anxieties, such as when an ill-prepared student sits down for his final exam. On this level, the remedy for fear is simple and straightforward, requiring no elaboration beyond repeating the Boy Scout motto: "Be Prepared!"

There are, of course, more lingering and deeply ingrained psychological anxieties, which, according to sources such as the *Vedas*, are primarily due to forgetting our true spiritual personalities. Forgetfulness of the real self creates a false consciousness wherein we identify with our physical bodies and material egos. Yet these material identities, such as "I am American," "I am an engineer," or "I am a woman," are external and transitory, while our essential personality is spiritual and eternal. By failing to distinguish clearly between our transcendental self and our physical and mental bodies, our minds can find no spiritual refuge from the inevitable disturbances and intimidation of the material energy. Thus, in times of distress or despondency, the mind attempts to relieve its pain either through absorbing itself in some sort of manic activity, or by desensitizing itself to distinctive personal existence. The latter option usually takes the form of chronic intoxication or enchantment with what is known as *mayavada*, or the idea that personality is only a temporary illusion.

Mayavadis, or impersonalists as they are known in the West, acknowledge our individuality but attribute it only to our material bodies, not the soul. Comparing the body to a vessel, they say that when "the vessel is broken the sky inside merges with the greater sky." But by simple reflection we can understand that the physical body can never be the basis of our true identity, for it is itself in flux, without any constant form. Science has determined that nearly all the organic matter comprising our bodies is replaced every two to three years. In fact, our bodies are principally composed of flowing liquids, so while our bodily form appears constant, it is really analogous to the form of a mountain stream. As the "permanence of form" of the stream is actually due to the shape of the gorge in the mountain and not to its "matter" (the water running through it), so the body itself is not permanent but is constantly reconstructed out of new matter. Obviously, then, the physical body is not the source of our individuality, for our personalities remain a continuing reality while all around us our bodies are being destroyed and recreated as they ingest, process, and dispose of matter. Therefore, it is not due to the body's imagined constancy that we have a clear sense of permanence and personality but, rather, because the spiritual self is ever-enduring and conscious.

Modern education offers little definitive knowledge of the spiritual self and its properties, but this failure should not open the door to fantasies of impersonalism or voidism. The philosopher Barrett makes an interesting point in this connection: "The obscurity of our idea of the self gives skeptics a seeming justification for trying to disprove its existence. But they confuse the reality of a thing and the extent of our knowledge of it. The reality of personal identity is so bedrock a fixture of our world that we hardly need single it out for special comment." Individuality is fundamental to our existence. We feel what happens to us directly, not to others, although we may empathize. I know immediately of my present feelings and that they are mine. This is what we mean by the "subjectivity" of the first person.

Impersonalism and Alienation

That the soul is personal, unique, and enduring is a wonderful truth standing against the false material and impersonal conceptions of life. In the dimmed light of conditioned consciousness, however, we not only lose sight of our own spiritual identity but also depersonalize others by seeing them as nothing more than the collection of roles they play. As Heidegger observed, in carrying out our everyday roles we tend to gloss over what is distinctly individual. Disconnecting with our deeper spiritual personality fosters a sense of alienation in our personal relations and pushes our minds towards indifference to others.

People are treated more as instruments to our ends, rather than ends in themselves, to be "used" for financial, emotional, or social advantage. Kant, who wrote at length on this subject, said that failing to provide assistance to those in distress was to sacrifice their ends to our own, treating them as having less validity than ourselves. This idea is graphically demonstrated in extreme cases such as murder, assault, or rape, where we treat the victim as of no account, as someone whose interests are to be sacrificed for our own. The philosopher Robert Enham explains, "The murderer or the thief pursues his own ends without any regard for the ends of his victim. He is willing to do anything that he can, regardless of the harm to others, in order to succeed in his projects. The victim is a mere opportunity and obstacle; he is not in any sense an object of respect."

In the same vein, the *Vedas* compare the attitudes characteristic of two distinctive mind-sets, the *asura* (impersonal-materialistic) and the *sura* (personal-spiritualistic). In this analysis, a *sura* is said to relate to individuals in a higher position with respect, to those in a lower position with compassion, and to his peers as a friend. Conversely, an *asura*, who has lost touch with his spiritual self, characteristically oppresses his subordinates, is envious of his superiors, and displays unbecoming pride in his accomplishments toward his equals. Naturally, most of us dwell somewhere between these two poles, but to develop spiritually we need to be keenly aware of the value of the individual personality, both in others and ourselves. Turning again to Enham: "There is a richness [in valuing the individual personality] which surpasses that of all other domains; and when we once appreciate it, we will appreciate freedom, otherness, and uniqueness in a manner that we never did before."

The impersonal mind-set also affects how we relate to our work and other activities, causing us to perform them simply for the result they deliver, rather than enjoying internal satisfaction from the activity itself. Alaisdair MacIntyre calls the former "alienated action" and distinguishes it from a "practice," which is where the *ends* of the action are internal to the action itself. In other words, "to practice" is to act for the sake of the activity itself. MacIntyre's example of a child learning to play chess illustrates the difference between acting for an external reward and acting for the satisfaction of exercising our imagination and analytical skills, rewards that are internal to the game itself. "The child has no particular desire to learn the game.

The child does, however, have a strong desire for candy and little chance of obtaining it. I therefore tell the child that if he will play chess with me once a week I will give him 50 cents worth of candy; moreover, I tell him that if he wins, he will receive an extra 50 cents worth of candy. Thus motivated, the child plays to win. But we hope that there will come a time when the child will find *in those goods specific to chess* a new set of reasons for trying to excel in whatever way the game of chess demands."

Psychologist Barry Schwartz adds that practices such as weaving, furniture making, cooking, or gardening may be done for a living, but this does not determine the character of these activities, because they possess their own internal properties. "But when each of these practices is reduced to an assembly line, the goods internal to them disappear. Assembly-line work is not a practice. A good assembly-line worker shows up for work and works just as hard and fast as he is told. What he is doing on the line doesn't matter."

Das Kapital has been justly and effectively discredited, but Marx did get this much right: work done only for securing a paycheck is alienating and depersonalizing, and modern industrialized societies frequently foster this type of work. This is not to say that many people don't find their jobs highly rewarding, only that countless individuals work principally for the pay they receive. Such work is impersonal and arbitrary because it has no intrinsic value; it could be readily exchanged as long as the reward remained intact.

The impersonal mind-set also lies at the heart of the growing concern over the commercialization of human relations. The expansion of commercialism is referred to as *economic imperialism,* where economic considerations encroach into areas that were previously noneconomic. Economist Fred Hirsch cites the example of education, which has now become largely an economic issue, with advanced education so closely tied to future earnings potential that one can almost put a dollar figure on certain degrees. Admittedly, education has always had some link to economic advantage, but, as Hirsch writes, it is no longer an overstatement to say that for most young people studying at the university level it has become the primary consideration. And the trend toward economic imperialism is by no means restricted to higher education. In fields as diverse as health care and professional sports, issues of financial gain are increasingly taking precedence over the more intrinsic rewards of activities, such as the exercise of compassion for the patient or simply the old-fashioned "love of the game."

Not surprisingly, some intellectuals, such as Nobel Prize-winning economist Gary Becker, do not consider economic imperialism to be a threat to our humanity; instead, they see it as part of our progressive social development. In their view, economic imperialism brings us closer to the true nature of the human species, for people can be best understood as "utility-maximizers," i.e., beings who, based on self-interest, rationally choose between life's alternatives. But to define ourselves as "utility-maximizers" is to assent to the charge that we are actuated only by desires to gratify the ego and the body, and to ignore the transcendental self that infuses life with meaning and true emotion.

Becker's crass analysis of the incentives for marriage and separation give evidence of the level of impersonalism inherent in such views. "By assumption, each marital 'strategy' produces a known amount of full wealth (i.e., money wealth and value of nonmarket time), and the opportunity set equals the set of full wealths produced by all conceivable marital strategies. The individual ranks all strategies by their full wealth and then chooses the highest. Even with certainty, a strategy with marriage, dissolution, and eventual remarriage might be preferred to all other strategies and anticipated at the time of the first marriage. Dissolution would be a response, perhaps, to the growing up of children or to the diminishing marginal utility of living with the same person, and would be a fully anticipated part of the variation in marital status over the life cycle." According to Becker, then, as "utility-maximizers," our decisions to marry, divorce, and even remarry are rooted in cost-benefit calculations designed to maximize our preferences. But does not defining human conduct in such terms "...constitute a major step in the making of 'unidimensional man,' a person who in every aspect is engaged in and guided by rational, economic consideration?"

Human beings are multi-faceted, and certainly our involvement in the material world demands certain cost-benefit analyses. Yet our core self is spiritual, and material influences cannot be allowed to obscure that truth from us. As the word *rational* comes from the Greek *ratio,* meaning in proportion or balanced, so we must maintain a balance between our natural drive for security and our deeper and more meaningful spiritual interests. From the Vedas we learn that our essence is pure soul and that the soul's natural activity is the exchange of loving service with the Supreme Soul. So it is that genuine spiritual activities have no trace of alienation, for they perfectly join together means and ends. As explained in the *Bhagavad-gita,* "One who is thus transcendentally situated at once realizes the Supreme Brahman and becomes joyful. He never laments nor desires to have anything. He is equally disposed toward every living entity. In that state he attains pure devotional service unto Me." This is Krishna telling Arjuna that the act of devotion is fully its own reward and that, in service to God, the true personality rejoices in the complete integration of love, desire, and action.

Alienation from Nature

Traditional cultures have always personalized nature, but modern thought disdains such views as pre-scientific mythology. More recently, however, modernity's impersonal paradigm has been found wanting, for although nature may possess certain machine-like properties, it is much more than a lifeless machine. Metaphors of nature as a clock or an engine tell us only part of the story, and taken too far, they trap us in an intellectual cul-de-sac. We may dream of a mathematical equation that, once uncovered, will render us masters of the universe but, accepting the Eastern view that the world around us is a direct expansion of God's energies, it would follow that finite entities would be limited in their capacity to dominate these divine energies. Buttressed by our technological successes, the modern impersonal view of nature has gained broad credibility. But the philosopher Huston Smith reminds us of the dangers of placing too much stock in our modern scientific view of the world. "When attention turns toward something, it turns away from something else. The triumphs of modern science—all in the material world, remember—have swung our attention toward the world's material aspects. The consequence—could anything be more natural?—has been progressive inattention to certain of the world's other properties. Stop attending to something and first we forget its importance; from there it is only a matter of time till one begins to wonder if it exists at all." Put another way, when we insist on seeing the world in impersonal terms, nature's God reciprocates by limiting our purview. Or as the Navajo Indians say, "I didn't believe it, so I couldn't see it."

Joseph Epes Brown contrasts the impersonal

mind-set predominant in modern society with the traditional outlook of Native Americans. "The strong sense of relationship pertains not only to members of a nuclear family, band, or clan, it also extends ever outwards to include all beings of the specific environment, the elements, and the winds, whether these beings, forms, or powers are what we call animate or inanimate. In native thought no such hard dichotomies exist." All such forms under creation were understood to be mysteriously interrelated; nothing existed in isolation. The intricate threads of the spider [the same metaphor is used in the ancient writings of India] were symbolic of the connectedness of the creation and the Creator. "Native Americans obviously observed that the threads of the web were drawn out from within the spider's very being." Furthermore, Native Americans believed spiritual knowledge could be found only through quieting and centering the mind, by directing one's consciousness within to discover "the still point in the turning universe." As such, Brown points out, "They also recognized that the threads forming the concentric circles were sticky, whereas the threads leading to the center were smooth."

Social, economic, and technological modernization has contributed mightily to the spiritual malaise that we have referred to here by the term alienation. Manfred Stanley eloquently describes, "At its most fundamental level, the diagnosis of alienation is based on the view that modernization forces upon us a world that, although baptized as real by science, is denuded of all humanly recognizable qualities; beauty and ugliness, love and hate, passion and fulfillment, salvation and damnation.... The world, once an 'enchanted garden,' has now become disenchanted, deprived of purpose and direction, bereft—in these senses—of life itself." Manfred goes on to explain how our contemporary "scientific worldview" makes it illegitimate to speak of evaluative and personal experiences as being "objectively" part of the world, pushing them "ever more into the province of dreams and illusions."

But we might suggest that the actual "dream" is the notion that the universe, filled as it is with beauty, love, and personality, has emerged from a primal condition entirely devoid of any qualities. And, it may be that the "illusion" is our posturing as the source of meaning and warmth in an indifferent space-time continuum, and considering ourselves "brave" for accepting this self-proclaimed reality.

One of India's most fascinating spiritual

literatures, the *Chaitanya Charitamrita*, describes the natural world as a dynamic expression of God's Personality, and as such, it is mysterious and filled with living spirit. In this light, alienation from nature is a by-product of alienation from God as the Supreme Friend. Developing a personal connection to the Soul of the Universe opens our eyes to the personal quality within all things in the creation. Thus inspired, we can burn away the haze of impersonalism through the potency of genuine spiritual practices. In this higher state of awareness, the fears that accompany our vision of the world as a lifeless machine are swiftly eradicated. Even the ordinary difficulties we face can be accepted with grace, and, rather than feeling helpless and insignificant, we understand that adversity is a personal challenge meant to help turn our minds toward the transcendental plane.

Impersonalism in the Afterlife

Personalism implies responsibility because it acknowledges the substantiality of the individual soul. Our personalities are real, not just an amalgamation of social and biological forces; therefore, we stand accountable to society and to God. Conversely, impersonalism offers an escape from the emotional pressure of personal identity and the effort to which it commits us. Spawned from weariness, it resembles the attitude of someone lying on the ground for fear of falling over, or of feigning death to deceive would-be attackers.

The impersonal mind-set culminates with the notion of merging with the infinite at death. This is the final escape from the pain of self, when one's unique being is totally obliterated through absorption. The individual loses his personal identity entirely, much as a raindrop becomes one with the sea into which it falls. There remains no memory, no awareness of individuality, and no purposive nature, as all personal qualities are lost forever. Yet the desire for the loss of selfhood is not characteristic of a healthy mental condition; in fact, modern psychology shows it to be the daily experience of many schizophrenics. The authors of *Modern Psychopathology* write, "A lack of personal identity is a notable feature in schizophrenic patients. In their early years, they rarely make references to themselves, if they speak at all. The term "I" frequently is lacking in their vocabulary. Presumably, this signifies their marked alienation, not only from others but from themselves."

Frequently, the impersonal account of transcendence uses the aforementioned analogy of a drop of water mingling with a larger mass of water to demonstrate how the self becomes one with the whole. However, mystics who lay claim to such experiences must return to their individuality to teach others what they have seen, a fact sufficient to show how he remains an independent center of thought and will *after* the experience as much as *before* it. Had his individuality really been substantially merged with impersonal spirit, no such return could be possible. Or, from another angle, if there is no self, then who is enlightened by this conclusion that there is no self? These inconsistencies are clear evidence that doctrines such as Buddhism are not really metaphysical but meant to teach a way of living, and as such, the Buddha emphasized practical values such as nonviolence, simplicity, and truthfulness.

Much of the allure of impersonalism emerges from our current experience of personal existence as a mixture of happiness and distress. Our frustration leads us to imagine that our eternal consciousness must be free from personal identity, for if it is the self who feels pain, then personality must have no place in the transcendental world of bliss. This is obviously faulty reasoning, for it ignores the possibility of a spiritual self that fully transcends the duality of this world. Furthermore, it is fair to say that impersonalism is not even a meaningful condition for the afterlife, a fact we are blinded to by our fear of personal spiritual identity. In this regard, Dr. Elton Trueblood raises the interesting question of what exactly would be required to avoid the absolute frustration of purpose that death seems to entail. Would it really solve our problem if our individual personality were lost forever, while our "spirit" is conserved as a drop of water is conserved when it falls into the ocean? To alter the common meaning of immortality so that it refers only to a depersonalized continuation of spirit is wholly unprofitable. "What we prize is not spirit in general, but concrete individuals. We cannot really understand God as Love or Good in the abstract, but only as an independent center of consciousness with His own particular activity. It is the individuality of spiritual life that is most precious to us." Even if a depersonalized immortality were accepted as having meaning, it would still seem less than wondrous to most thoughtful people, because *they would not be there* to experience it!

The Sanskrit term for spiritual life is *vaikuntha,* which is a compound word formed from *vai* (without) and *kuntha* (anxiety). Conversely, material life is characterized by anxiety, which is the recurring symptom of forgetfulness of our personal spiritual identity. Material identification covers our true self, as a brilliant jewel is obscured by dried clay.

Presently, our blissful and fearless spiritual nature is clouded by the twin myths of materialism and impersonalism. Materialism's claim is that we are simply by-products of these temporary physical bodies, while impersonalism calls for the negation of the self through an imaginary merging process. But we do not emerge out of electro-chemical activity; neither are we a hallucination, momentarily floating above a limitless sea of impersonal energy. These are misguided notions that take shape under the influence of weariness and frustration. Lord Krishna explains in the poetic language of the *Bhagavad-Gita,* "Never was there a time when I did not exist, nor you, nor all these kings. Nor in the future shall we ever cease to be." Firmly embracing this truth will lift us above the fears that give rise to impersonal conceptions of life and allow us to experience the peacefulness and clarity of mind that is the foundation of spiritual insight.

Chapter Four

Anger and Letting Go

Having discussed attachment and fear, we now turn to what Eastern spiritual traditions identify as the third disturbing agent of the mind, anger. The destructive force of anger is well known to us all as it spills out into our homes as domestic fighting and abuse, onto our highways as callous and menacing drivers, and across cities and nations as riots and wars. The awesome sight of a mushroom cloud rushing skyward offers an indelible image of the force of our collective anger unleashed against a common foe.

Commonly, anger grows out of frustration. We become incensed when people or events refuse to follow our dictates and desires; our plane is late, our child is disobedient, someone treats us rudely, and so forth. The potential causes of anger are almost unlimited, but a common thread runs through nearly all our irritation – something has not gone the way that we wanted. Not surprisingly, because we see ourselves as the injured party, our anger generally seems to us a justifiable response. But however fitting our anger may appear subjectively, it is nevertheless a heavy price to pay, for surrendering to our anger not only disrupts our minds and puts us in jeopardy at the present moment, it also has long-term effects.

In this chapter, we will consider two qualities that are indispensable for liberating ourselves from the agitating energy of anger. The first is patience, and the second is humility, which also includes what we call "embracing ambiguity." A third attribute, forgiveness, is obviously related to overcoming feelings of anger, but as it is a much-discussed topic in many religious and social forums, we will not address it here.

Patience and Enthusiasm

Sometimes we are led to believe that if something is good, then more of it must be better. But this not always the case. Excess can also lead to a morbid intensification that distorts a quality or characteristic to the point where it manifests its negative aspects. To illustrate this concept, consider the natural complement between enthusiasm and patience. Each is a positive and productive trait, yet each possesses the potential to disrupt and destroy if pushed beyond its appropriate limits.

Patience tempers our anxiousness and frustration and, as such, is critical to achieving any meaningful goal, for we all know from experience that success rarely falls out of the sky and into our laps. No question, Grandmother was right when she told us repeatedly, "Rome wasn't built in a day." In romantic affairs, for example, we know that relationships need to grow in their own time. We ask for trouble when we demand too much from the other party before they are prepared to reciprocate, and long-term vows such as marriage require caution and careful consideration. Examples of the virtue of patience can also be drawn from the world of sports, where experts often speak of how a star athlete "lets the game come to him." This means he does not impatiently impose his will to excel but responds to the timing and flow of the contest as a whole. In the same way, anyone who has developed a skill to a high level of accomplishment has experienced seeing a novice attempting to mimic a true expert and looking foolish in the process. A beginner may try to incorporate the style and flourish of a polished athlete, imagining that desire alone is adequate to the task, but developing real expertise requires the application of enthusiasm with great perseverance.

Thus, patience is indispensable to our personal development, but when debilitating thoughts and emotions undermine the sense of self, patience becomes perverted into its negative forms, such as lethargy or indifference. No longer energized by enthusiasm, patience erodes into apathy and a loss of interest in the important affairs of life. Often such lack of interest is connected, as both cause and effect, to frequent drug or alcohol use. Among the Sioux Indians, such a mental state of total discouragement with life is call *tawal ye sni* and is characterized by thoughts of suicide and helplessness.

Clearly, to be successful in any area of endeavor, a sense of value must attach be attached to our efforts. In the natural mind, enthusiasm, which is the mentally invigorated state that infuses one's thoughts and actions with energy and hope, acts as the natural complement of patience. We are conscious of our nature as active, dynamic beings, and this awareness is seamlessly interwoven with an awareness that the results of our actions are, in the final sense, dependent on a higher power. This integrated vision prevents the illusion of pride and arrogance from arising when we "gain," as it likewise inhibits unwarranted self-deprecation if we "lose," even after giving our best effort. Thereby freed of anxiety for loss or gain, we can focus on the activity with calm intensity, concerned with "what" we are doing, not "how" we are doing. This perspective allows us to settle into our "equilibrium state." Famous ballplayer Ken Griffey, Jr. captured the spirit of this attitude in his response to the question of how he always appears so unflappable, even maintaining his cool-headed demeanor when hitting a crucial homerun or making a game-saving catch. He explained that by knowing how much of sports (and of life, we might add) is beyond his direct control, he doesn't get "too up" about his successes, nor "too down" in times of failure. He takes both in stride, avoiding the emotional roller coaster ride and concentrating on doing the best he can. Successful athletes, like others of great accomplishment, work with a steady determination, where the energy of the will is balanced with the quiet strength of patience.

When the mind is free from egoism and apathy, the two tendencies (patience and enthusiasm) blend and balance one another to create a happy mental outlook and pleasing behavior. Knowing that one is not the supreme controller mitigates the self-centered egoism of passion, while apathy is avoided by an understanding that, as spiritual beings, our actions truly are meaningful. Although in one sense we are the "architects of our own destiny," this truth is joined to the realization that we must respond calmly and humbly to the disruptions and pitfalls in our lives, without frustration or anger, for we are not the center of the universe. The power of the will should not be stifled or underestimated but, rather, expressed with acknowledgement of our legitimate place in the greater reality.

Humility

Humility—a quality that is nowadays often misunderstood and even maligned. Although humility informs much of the Christian ideal, Western culture has become largely neglectful of its power and importance as a human value. Part of this neglect can be attributed to our society's currently dominant worldview, which has been identified as a blend of naturalism and the will to control. (Naturalism contends that anything in our experience can be reduced to its material components and, as such, it fortifies science's effort to predict and control nature, primarily through the use of mathematics.)

The scientific worldview became prominent during the 17th and 18th centuries in Europe, as Enlightenment thinkers argued that reason is the highest faculty in man and that through the free pursuit of science, we could increase our comfort and safety. Out of natural science, they predicted, would come technological advances that would more effectively satisfy men's needs, or in Francis Bacon's words, would "ease man's estate." The determined scientific mind could subordinate nature, our "cruel stepmother," and man's health and prosperity would be assured. Or as Descartes roundly asserted, "Science will make man master and possessor of nature."

In many ways the Enlightenment vision developed as its authors had hoped. More than three centuries later, science is an integral and highly respected part of the industrialized world, and with increasing global economic development, it is becoming more central to the lives of people in less industrialized societies as well. However, there are numerous reservations about the benefits of scientific progress. For instance, concern is widespread over the unintended consequences of some of our scientific creations (the Frankenstein phenomenon), such as environmental degradation, irreversible biological alterations, or wholesale destruction through the use of technologically sophisticated weapons of war.

These important concerns have been much debated and discussed. At the same time, the scientific worldview's permeation of our culture has, in the eyes of many observers, exacted a heavy psychological toll as well. Philosopher Huston Smith addresses this issue by reminding us of the risk we run by placing excessive faith in a worldview that is limited by its reliance on empiricism, that is, knowledge received through our senses and their extensions. "The exceptional power-to-control that modern science has made possible has made us reach out insistently, perhaps even desperately if we feel we are on a treadmill, for ever-increasing control. This outreach has forged a new epistemology wherein knowledge that facilitates control is honored to the neglect of its alternatives. This has constricted our view of the way things are, including what it means to be fully human." Psychiatrist George Anastaplo agrees, pointing out in his article on the importance of learning from nature that we have paid a steep price by living for the last four centuries under the assumption that nature is something to be conquered, to be used, to be exploited. "If nature is something to be conquered and harnessed," he explains, "it is difficult to regard her as a master or guide."

Approaching nature as an object to be controlled robs us of our capacity to fully appreciate nature as God's instrument for teaching us about our own spirituality. Speaking on the essence of Navajo religious tradition, an Indian woman explains how her people's worldview is shaped by their profound respect for nature. "The land is our Bible. Every feature has a name and a story and is sacred, just as every animal or plant has a 'way,' its own particular means of contributing, its right to be there, which must be respected." Much of a Navajo's energies are devoted to keeping on good terms with the elements and one's fellow creatures, to "being in harmony with everything—yourself, all the living things, the air, Father Sky, the moon, and on and on." Regrettably, for many people interaction with nature is limited by the modern urban environment in which they dwell. Respect for nature is easily set aside when the sight of her is lost, and manifestations of nature in growing things (woods and meadows, crops and flowers, to say nothing of all kinds of animals) are now largely concealed from view. Nature is also concealed from view by current scientific theories, because the explanations of the world constructed by modern science cannot be put in terms of everyday observations, even as rough approximations or crude analogies. "Only mathematics can be used to describe what the scientists (especially the physicists) construct, and these descriptions, however ratified they may be in common opinion by astounding technological marvels, are simply incomprehensible to most of the community."

Related to this eclipse of nature is what has happened to the status of the divine, at least in the public discourse of intellectuals. Anastapol writes of how, at one time, a useful way to talk about nature was to talk about the divine. "Certainly the divine provided standards, guidance, and goals; it provided a reliable context within which the arts, including medicine, could work. It was once considered natural, even among many skeptics, that the divine should be publicly respected. But such respect is considered by all too many intellectuals as repressive, as an illusion, as hypocritical, as a kind of wish fulfillment, or as mere fearfulness. Nevertheless, a respect for nature, in the old-fashioned sense, and a respect for religion do go hand in hand."

Under the banner of naturalism, our contemporary intellectual milieu considers the implication of God in natural phenomenon to be unsophisticated or even superstitious, a quaint vestige of primitive yearnings. But before the mysteries and power of nature, with its estimated 8 billion stars in each of 8 billion galaxies, a measure of humility is actually the most rational position. Science and its offspring, technology, have brought us many advantages in terms of material comfort. But the modern scientific worldview has also "constricted our view of the way things are, especially what it means to be fully human." To see nature principally as an adversary that needs to be, according to Bacon, "put on a rack and forced to reveal her secrets" causes us to lose much of our sense of wonder and natural humility. It is this loss that writer Saul Bellow refers to when he entreats us to "Rediscover the magic of the world under the debris of modern ideas." In traditional cultures, people looked first to God's grace for their well-being and understood divine blessings to be obtainable through acts such as meditation, prayer, religious rituals, and obedience to Higher Law. But, again from Bellow, "It is a long time since the knees were bent in piety."

Although composed thousands of years ago,

India's *Srimad Bhagavatam* narrates a story relevant to the current tension between materialistic and spiritualistic worldviews. In an ancient kingdom, Hiranyakashipu, a powerful but arrogant ruler, enjoyed declaring publicly that he had no use for the idea of God. Ironically, Hiranyaksipu's son, Prahlada, held a firm belief in the Supreme Being, Vishnu, and refused to submit to his father's demands that he abandon his theistic convictions. The king's frustration at his son's unwavering faith eventually turned to fury, and he declared him to be an obstinate fool (*stabdham manda-atman*) who disrupts the family (*kula-bheda-kara*). Hiranyakashipu demanded to know where Prahlada received his gentle strength, but when his son told him that the source of all strength was God, the king became even further enraged and threatened to kill his own son. He challenged Vishnu to save Prahlada from his wrath, and mockingly asked that if God is everywhere, why is He not in the column before him. The king smashed the column with his fist, and "From within the pillar came a fearful sound, which appeared to crack the covering of the universe." Just as modern scientists smashed the atom to release the fearsome power of nuclear fission, a most terrifying form of Vishnu rushed out of the pillar and destroyed Hiranyakashipu.

Blinded by his pride and anger, Hiranyakashipu failed to appreciate the spiritual qualities and inner strength of his own son, and, like so many who are self-impressed by their sense of material accomplishment, Hiranyakashipu mistook humility for weakness. In fact, true humility is a trait possible only for the strongest at heart, as the succinct poetry of the Tao Te Ching reminds us: "He who stands on tiptoe does not stand firm. He who possesses the Tao does not call attention to his successes."

Another important aspect of developing genuine humility and gaining the insight it affords us is what we have termed "embracing ambiguity." An ancient Chinese poem speaks of accepting with grace the inherent ambiguity of life:

"No lake so still but that it has its wave.
No circle so perfect but that it has its blur.
I would change things for you if I could;
As I can't, you must take them as they are."

Life is not always neat and tidy. Most of us can sympathize with American chess masters Paul Morphy and Bobby Fischer, who both so preferred the perfectly clear-cut and logically ordered world of chess that they "turned their backs on the messy confusion of the 'real' world."

Undoubtedly, as the poem above suggests, there is a certain vagueness and uncertainty in the very nature of our world. The respected scientist Jacob Bronowski explains in *The Ascent of Man,* "The essence of the world itself is more delicate and more fugitive than we can catch in the butterfly nets of our senses." Although we devise more precise instruments to observe nature with more fineness, the final images remain as uncertain as ever. "We fire electrons at the smallest object, yet they only trace out its outline like a knife-thrower at a fair. Perfect images are still as remote as the distant stars...we seem to be in search of a goal that lurches away from us every time we come in sight of it." Bronowski concludes, "Errors cannot be taken out of observations; they are inextricably bound up in the nature of human knowledge." In Sanskrit this relation between our senses and the world is known as *karana patava,* or the inevitable imperfection of sense perception. We live and move within a zone of tolerance, so to speak, where absolute precision gives way to what is adequate and necessary to successful functioning. Even in the seemingly simple and orderly world of grade school mathematics (what to speak of calculus or the equations of quantum mechanics), we can never know *exactly* what is the circumference or area of a circle, since the function (multiplier) *pi* is itself indeterminate.

In the realm of our language we find almost constant ambiguity, for while numbers are signs (they stand directly for something), words are symbolic, and therefore much of the meaning we gather from verbal communication is equivocal. Although on the negative side this can lead to misunderstandings and disputes, it also prevents language from becoming too sterile and allows us to share in a richness of meaning through our varying perspectives. Subtlety is a characteristic, Huston Smith writes, "...that makes language fertile and capable of reaching into every crevice of the human soul." This is the key to appreciating the concept of "embracing ambiguity," recognizing that not everything can or should be "nailed down." It is often preferable and rewarding to allow things to remain open, to not insist on resolution or "closure," but to draw our senses in and let answers and direction emerge from within.

This approach conflicts with many of our cultural patterns, which are founded on a linear view of space and time. Even our expressions reveal our bias toward the "line and the grid." We speak of "getting things straightened out" and "toeing the line," while someone who is incoherent "talks in circles." Even the physical gesture for being out of touch with reality is a circular hand motion around the ear. Contrast this with India's Vedic culture, where the sacred form of the circle is expressed through round mandalas that adorn ancient temples, and pilgrims circumambulate their holy shrines as offerings of respect. Their non-linearity is joined to their view of the entire cosmos, which is seen as being filled with graceful forms in flowing motion. Their universal vision culminates in the supremely beautiful planet, Goloka Vrndavana, which is shaped like the whorl of a blooming lotus flower and is presided over by Sri Krishna, Who stands in three-fold bending form. In the Vedic culture, along with nearly all non-Western traditions, time as well as space is seen as non-linear. Just as the four seasons pass and return on our earthly globe, cosmic time is seen as gliding across massive cycles of ages, which disappear and re-emerge perpetually. In Western traditions such as the Judeo-Christian, on the other hand, time is generally conceived of as linear, moving to the future in straight track progression from a distant past that is never to be seen again.

Professor Barre Toelken writes of this distinction in his essay on Native Americans, *How Many Sheep*

Will It Hold? "In the West we think of logic as being in straight lines: **A** plus **B** equals **C**. We look forward to the conclusion of things, we plan into the future, as though time were a sort of train track along which we move toward certain predictable goals. We learn to find each other in the house or city by learning the intersection of straight lines. We have it all neatly separated and categorized. For most Native American groups, almost the reverse is true—things are brought together. Instead of separating into categories of this sort, family groups sit in circles, meetings are in circles, dances are often in circles, especially the dances intended to welcome and include people."

The quality of humility is highly esteemed in Eastern thought because it gives clarity and freedom to our thoughts. The opacity of pride is symptomatic of material consciousness, where we live in the illusion that we are acting independently of God's grace. This is the source of much of the frustration that disrupts our minds and, left unchecked, transforms into irritation, anger, or even rage. Psychologist Mihaly Csikszentmihalyi speaks to this in describing the state of mind he calls "non-self-conscious individualism:"

"Such individuals are bent on doing their best in all circumstances, yet they are not concerned primarily with advancing their own interests. Because they are intrinsically motivated in their actions, they are not easily disturbed by external threats. With enough psychic energy free to observe and analyze their surroundings objectively, they have a better chance of discovering in them new opportunities for action. Narcissistic individuals, who are mainly concerned with protecting their own self, fall apart when the external conditions turn threatening. The ensuing panic prevents them from doing what they must do; their attention turns inward in an effort to restore order in consciousness, and not enough remains to negotiate outside reality."

The material ego, empty of all substance except its vain attempt to transform all things in heaven and on earth into means for its preservation, recoils from the medicine of patience and humility, insisting that frustration can only be overcome by more and improved control. But we are not the supreme controller, and just as a physician may do everything possible to save a patient, yet still the patient dies, so our actions may not produce the outcome we hope for. Patience and humility enable us to accept such frustration without self-centered pride or self-indulgent lamentation. They permit us to do what needs to be done with all our energy and ability, yet without demanding that the results be in accord with our personal desires and preconceptions. As intrinsic qualities of the soul, patience and humility act in tandem to free us from anger and false pride, show us our place in the natural order, and open the path to greater spiritual awareness.

Chapter Five

The Way of Nature

The world seems filled with endless variety, as countless objects, animate and inanimate, bustle and bloom about us. Yet amidst all the wondrous differences and complexities stimulating our senses and invigorating our minds, we intuit an underlying simplicity to nature, that she somehow weaves her infinite patterns with but a small collection of threads. In fact, ancient teachings describe nature in just this way, as an elaborate fabric woven from three primal strands. Known as *gunas* in Sanskrit, they form the essential psychological qualities of all natural phenomena, mixing together to create the tone or hue of our mental experiences in the same way that combinations of red, blue, and yellow give rise to the nearly limitless array of colors.

The three qualities are known as *sattva* (goodness), *rajas* (passion), and *tamas* (ignorance), and our thoughts and feelings take on certain qualities as we place them (consciously or unconsciously) in contact with mixtures of these modes. The idea of the modes of nature is found throughout Eastern spiritual teachings, such as in the famous Chinese poem the *Tao Te Ching*, where Lao-tsu speaks of the Tao as the subtle "way" or "mode" in which all actions and events unfold.

Looking at the specific qualities of each mode, we find *sattva* (goodness) to be the way of mental serenity and harmony, characterized by the idea of balance. Living in balance, either in the case of an individual or an entire society, conveys the importance of moderation in the conduct of our affairs. For example, when our endeavor for economic development becomes too feverish, we ignore the fragile interdependency of life forms in our environment; thus, nature's carefully crafted ecosystems and entire species are threatened with extinction. Similarly, in our own lives, greed or excessive desire for sexual pleasure, for example, can carry us from the path of righteousness and deprive us of our natural contentment. From the Native Indian we learn the term *koyanasquatsi*, meaning "life out of balance." It is a concept that neatly captures the state of disturbance that ensues when a person or society loses respect for moderation and the natural order.

The mode of passion, *rajas*, is the second of nature's foundational qualities. *Rajas*, as the outward rushing impetus, exhibits itself through externally directed activity. It is the spirit of accumulation, the desire for fame, and the craving for power over others. In its untempered form, *rajas* drives one to seize whatever lies outside the self for the purpose of controlling or enjoying. Akin to what Jung labels the libido, it compels us to range through the world in search of satisfaction.

The quality of passion arises when one's natural sense of completeness is lost due to mental disequilibrium. Because one dominated by the mode of passion feels a need to "become whole" through enjoying or possessing something in the world around him, he attempts to subjugate the world to his own will. This necessitates dividing it into manageable parts, then seeing these "parts" as potential objects to be controlled or enjoyed. (This tendency obviously reflects the strategy of modern science and its impressive use of analysis and reductionism.)

When *rajas* is active, we grasp for the fruit of our actions, invigorated by the notion that attaining it will satisfy our longing. Unfortunately, we are often unable to secure the objects of our desires, and even when they are acquired, the satisfaction they provide is limited. It is this gap between hope and reality that creates frustration in the mind of the *rajasic* actor.

Ideally, such frustration acts as a signal, as a lesson to inspire us toward the superior way of goodness. An attentive mind, tired of the pattern of endeavoring to acquire things that do not truly fulfill, comes to value the wisdom of moderation and the enjoyment of simple, pure activities. Unfortunately, frustration often leads to renewed efforts to enjoy in the same manner that produced the original frustration, and so we tread the same path again, failing to understand that we are "hoping against hope."

The mode of *rajas* is efficient at reproducing this cycle, because it creates and sustains the mental image that we are independent actors who must generate our own pleasures. So when *rajas* becomes prominent, we feel compelled to acquire what is needed for our personal gratification with little acknowledgment of other factors or options. Thus, the self-centered egoism of *rajas* serves as the basis for activity directed toward all varieties of personal gain. When functioning in this mode, the individual is often invigorated by a sense of superiority and a spirit of enjoyment, seeing the world as essentially a place constructed for his dominion and pleasure. Personalities renowned for their almost superhuman drive for conquest and control, such as Napolean Bonaparte or Alexander the Great, were exceptionally powerful *rajasic* actors. Predictably, however, they also frequently suffered from bouts of abnormal depression and despair.

When untempered by the other modes (particularly goodness), *rajas* can produce states of manic excitement. A psychiatrist's observation of a manic patient reveals such a mental condition to be unadulterated *rajas*. "The patient is in a constant state of activity, commencing a new occupation at every moment and immediately abandoning it in favor of another. He is never still but exhibits a continual press of activity. He talks rapidly and without intermission. His attention is caught by every trivial object, and just as soon diverted again. He is generally abnormally cheerful and pleased with himself, though the mood changes to anger at the slightest provocation." Although clearly excessive, can we not recognize some of our own tendencies in this description?

The third mode is *tamas,* or ignorance. The quality of *tamas* transforms the frustration and disdain of *rajas* into anger and cynicism. Attachment and desire become heavy and dominating when linked to the mode of ignorance, for they become imbued with fear and anger. When *tamas* grows exceptionally powerful, it can induce irrationality, rage, and even madness. Whereas *rajas* relentlessly compels the mind to seek completeness in objects of desire and self-centered relations, *tamas* engenders apathy and depression by draining the world of any positive appeal. In so doing, it is the agent of drug and alcohol addiction, of suicide, and of yielding to dull compulsion.

When the mode of *tamas* manifests in an extreme form, the properties of passion and goodness are conspicuous by their absence, as illustrated by the following description from the *Psychology of Insanity*. "The patient sits in the corner with expressionless face and head hanging down, making no attempt to occupy himself in any way, evincing no interest in anything that goes on around him, and apparently noticing nothing. The patient is completely inert and makes no use of his mental faculties [not because he has none, but] because he has no self-interest or desires. The whole external world for him is an object unworthy of the expenditure of any mental energy. He is without interest, hopes, plans, or ambition." Certainly such excessive lethargy is rare, but again, can we not recognize some of the same tendencies that affect us from time to time?

To help illustrate how the mode of ignorance operates on our thoughts and feelings, we can consider how it is reflected in the physical domain as the principle of entropy (Newton's Second Law of Thermodynamics). This principle states that matter naturally tends toward disorganization and randomness if not acted upon by some higher ordering principle (such as human will or genetic coding instructions). In a more vivid and personal style, India's classic writings describe how the demigod Shiva, who is the ruler of the mode of ignorance, governs the *tamasic* principle. Accompanied by his ghostly associates, he presides over all activities of destruction, including physical, mental, and even spiritual (as impersonalism, or loss of the self). His power is contrasted to Brahma's, the lord of *rajas*, whose creative intelligence engineers the construction of the three worlds. The hopelessness and despair of disintegration, however, finally and inevitably swallow up Brahma's creative masterpiece, as

Shiva's dance of universal destruction shatters all form and order in creation.

Another means to visualize nature's three qualities is to imagine various scenarios characterizing the properties of each of the modes. For example, an unclean and inappropriately dark atmosphere, especially where people are indulging in intoxication or other self-destructive activities, is indicative of a *tamasic* environment. In contrast, the quality of *rajas* would predominate in scenes of excited enjoyment, intense sense stimulation, or anticipation of gain, such as a busy session on the floor of the New York Stock Exchange. And finally, a peaceful natural setting, such as a calm lake surrounded by lush vegetation and picturesque mountains, would represent the mode of *sattva*. Under the influence of goodness, the mind senses the harmonious flow of the natural world and feels connected to the deeper self, for *sattva* is the way of lucidity and insight, where the perception of eternal truths begins to emerge.

It should be pointed out that although we may enter into an environment dominated by one of the three modes, our presence alone does not compel us to accept the mentality of that mode. The quality of our consciousness is formed by the entirety of our past choices and activities, and attraction for the different modes and their combinations is based on this long history, or karma. For example, a police officer may patrol a derelict area without feeling any compulsion to participate in the activities prevalent there. On the other hand, a reformed alcoholic, who still harbors a strong desire to consume liquor as a means to forget the world and cover his pain, would likely feel the strong pull of *tamas*.

Will Power

Knowledge of how the three modes interact is a wonderful asset in understanding any situation, be it personal, social, spiritual, etc. For example, consider the long-standing debate over where to place responsibility for anti-social behavior. Is a murderer also a victim of a society that mistreated him? Or does the blame fall squarely on his shoulders? Is his choice of action, in the most important sense, personal and elective?

While interesting and credible arguments can be delivered from both sides, insight into how the three modes weave together helps us unravel the tension between the two views. Stated briefly, overemphasis on the "social context" as the determinant of individual conduct would be symptomatic of *tamas*, while attributing complete responsibility to the person as a "doer" and neglecting structural influences would reflect the zealous nature of *rajas*.

For a number of years, influential schools of psychological thought have stressed the power of the social and developmental contexts, almost to the exclusion of individual responsibility for control and change. Sigmund Freud wrote in 1935, "The deeply-rooted belief in psychic freedom and choice is quite unscientific and must give way before the claims of a determinism which governs mental life." Behaviorist B.F. Skinner also endorsed this view, claiming that human actions are simply a reaction to various external stimuli. Although these specific views may appear extreme, their basic outlook is widely shared as an explanation for human conduct and illustrates the deemphasis on individual will that occurs when the mode of *tamas* becomes dominant. Allan Wheelis nicely makes this point: "Knowledgeable moderns put their backs to the couch and in so doing may fail to put their shoulders to the wheel. As will has been devalued, so has courage; for courage can exist only in the service of will. In our understanding of human nature we have gained determinism: lost determination."

At the same time, an individual is genuinely constrained by the structure of the systems (social, economic, educational, etc.) he lives within, as they exert real power to limit possibilities and determine outcomes. It is no accident that the term "hero" refers to one who rises above adverse circumstances to accomplish a goal, and "heroic" indicates the extraordinary quality of such endeavors.

Seeing how the two modes pull at one another when set in opposition, the balanced perspective, which acknowledges the dynamic interplay of the various influences, would reflect the *sattvic* position. The entire range of current institutions that influence the development of a person (family, educational, criminal justice, etc.) are shaped by the thoughts and actions of leaders and members of society. As these institutions are flawed, so are they capable of oppressing and discouraging those who dwell within them. For example, Allan Bloom writes elegantly of the sterility of the modern family and its inability to communicate a spiritual vision of the world to its children. "The dreariness of the modern family's spiritual landscape passes belief. It is as monochrome and unrelated to those who pass through it as are the barren steppes frequented by nomads who take their mere subsistence and move on. The delicate fabric of the civilization into which the successive generations are woven has unraveled, and children are raised, not educated."

The vantage from the mode of goodness reveals how these contextual factors (family, society, etc.) must be taken into account without neglecting the power of the human will to "take matters in hand." Importantly, however, the *sattvic* position should not to be confused with a compromise stance, taken up simply as an easy escape from an intellectual conundrum. In fact, rather than being a short cut, full understanding in the mode of goodness does not come cheaply. It requires direct perception of our entanglement in the web of action and desire, a realization that is gained by the practice of self-restraint and spiritual reflection.

To illustrate this last idea, consider how our actions and choices unfold according to the principle of karma. Our karma unfolds in a "path dependent" manner, meaning that each and every decision incrementally moves a person along a "path" already carved out by previous actions. (Obviously, reincarnation would allow this development to span successive lifetimes). Path dependency can be pictured as a steel ball bearing careening down a board filled with rows and columns of pegs. With each successive contact the ball bounces only slightly to the left or right, so its present position is the cumulative result of all its accumulated "choices." Nevertheless, it can re-direct itself at any time and steadily move to an entirely new section of the board. So it is with human actors. We are able to significantly shift our futures into entirely new directions, but such movement requires determination and commitment to the correct decision at each opportunity.

The Interaction of the Three Modes

The three qualities of nature represent distinct psychological tendencies, yet they are wound together as separate strands forming a single rope. In this way, the distinctive properties of the three modes play out within the greater unity of the natural world. Patterns of *sattva, rajas,* and *tamas* create the ever-changing tapestry of our mental and physical environments, and we interact with these gross and subtle textures according to our own inclinations and values. For example, the *Bhagavad-gita* explains that desire (*rajas*) and hate (*tamas*) form an interconnected pair. Desire pushes the mind toward objects or ideas, and attachment arises out of the contact with them. Conversely, aversion pushes the mind away from other objects or ideas, or even the same ones at a different time. The Lebanese mystic Kahil Gibran wrote of this dual nature of attachment and aversion, "But I say unto you, joy and sorrow are inseparable. Together they come, and when one sits alone with you at your board, remember that the other is asleep at your bed."

Seen in this light, attachment is recognized to be aversion's companion, not its opposite. Since both depend on a false sense of the self as an independent enjoyer, they exist in relation to one another as two sides of the same coin. Failing to recognize this, our minds are relentlessly pressured by the force of attraction and repulsion. It is this ongoing process that disrupts the natural mental equilibrium, or *samata,* of the self. While moral and ethical restraints are important in gradually strengthening the mind's resolve and steadfastness, it is only genuine spiritual vision that reveals how passion and ignorance work in tandem to agitate the mind.

Perhaps most commonly associated with this concept of the dual nature of opposites is the Chinese tradition, symbolized by the integrated circle of yin and yang. This ancient symbol represents how polarized forces are inextricably bound up, each relying on the other for its identity or being. The terms yin and yang mean literally the "dark side" and the "sunny side" of a hill, and they refer both to categories (e.g., female and male) and to forces (the life-breath of earth and the life-breath of heaven).

This relativity of all attributes is the first great principle of Chinese Taoism, which teaches that nothing in this world is absolute or independent. For example, a distance is neither long nor short, but merely longer or shorter than something else that we accept as a standard. In the *Chuang Tzu* the story is told of a wren, who, upon hearing that some birds fly hundreds of miles without stopping, declared such a thing to be out of the question. "You all know very well that the furthest one can get by the most tremendous effort is that elm tree there; and even this is not always certain every time. All these stories about flying hundreds of miles are pure nonsense." The *Chuang Tzu* explains that those with a greater intellectual embrace than the wren see not only the relativity of distance, but also the relativity of all attributes of this world.

The relation of opposites as twin aspects of a single principle is also nicely portrayed in a classical Chinese poem. "What is the nature of the perturbations that cause the loss of the quiet mind?

They are grief and joy, delight and anger, desire and greed for gain. Put these all away and your mind will return to its purity. For such is the mind that only peace and stillness are good for it. Do not fret, do not let yourself be perturbed, and accord with nature will come unsought."

In India's famous *Bhagavad-gita,* contact between the living consciousness and *maya,* or inert matter, is the origin of all duality. When the *atma,* or life force, is embedded in the material energy, the initial duality (body and self) is generated. This primary "separateness" further takes root as the urge to measure and name whatever enters our field of experience. Thus duality arises under the influence of the mode of passion, and our propensity to objectify and control matter fuels this appetite for dividing and counting. Although we are tiny in comparison to the world around us, we still sense our innate superiority (as consciousness) to the "will-less" material energy. However, under the influence of *rajas* and *tamas* we misunderstand the true nature of our superior status. Because dualities such as attachment and aversion arise from the false sense of self that arises from *rajas,* we must de-link ourselves from its influence and connect the mind to the mode of *sattva.* From the *sattvic* perspective, dualities are accurately seen as external to the self, and our minds are free to experience their normal, happy condition of clarity and peace.

The twin illusions of hankering and lamenting are clear examples of how *rajas* and *tamas* disrupt our natural serenity. As we have seen, the way of *rajas* is desire, which often takes the form of craving for money, sex, or power. Born from the mode of passion, these material aspirations are future-oriented in that we hanker to obtain what we do not yet possess (or to secure what we do have into the future). In this way, *rajas* directs our attention toward "the next" as we anticipate tomorrow's satisfactions. The old admonition "Don't forget to stop and smell the roses" is an apt warning to a person striving under the influence of *rajas*.

Lamentation, on the other hand, binds the mind to the past and what might have been. By contact with *tamas*, our will power is subdued and we mourn lost opportunities and "the way it could have been." Because the focus is on events in the past, there is an inherent helplessness to lamentation, wherein "the world has spoken" and the self is left only to pine. It is a perspective that induces a sense of victimization and the tendency to curse the darkness rather than light a candle.

Unfortunately, when our mind vacillates

between these two poles, its spiritual strength is depleted. Instead of focusing on the present moment and all it has to offer, our thoughts are diverted to either our wishes or memories. Conversely, the mode of goodness directs our attention to the present and we appreciate activity performed simply for the satisfaction of "doing the right thing." In its fullest expression, such activity develops into living for the pleasure of God and becomes timeless, that is, free from our pre-occupation with the past or future. Interestingly, one of J.D. Salinger's well-known stories describes the liberating experience of doing our life's work in the mode of spiritual goodness. The character Zooey explains to Franny that he has come to realize the meaning of the advice they had received from their mentor, Seymour. Seymour had intimated to them that to find real happiness you needed to do whatever you do for the satisfaction of Jesus. In the *Gita* this consciousness is explained as *karma yoga,* or working for the pleasure of God, free from the control of material desire.

Certainly, all that we learn through experience is vital to our personal growth. We do not want to dwell in the past, but we do want to use our experience as a living part of our present decision-making process. In the mode of goodness, the conviction of our current decision is not weakened by despondency over past losses or failures. Our past does not intimidate us, instead we integrate our experience into our deliberations to form a mature and realistic outlook. Once we understand how *tamas* entangles the mind in fantasies of what might have been, while *rajas* places us in a dream world of wishes and longings, we can center our thoughts on the simple reality of what lies directly before us.

Pleasure and Pain

Over two millennia ago, Plato wrote of the pursuit of pleasure, "How singular is the thing called pleasure, and how curiously related to pain, which might be thought to be the opposite of it; for they are never present at the same instant, yet he who pursues either is generally compelled to take the other; their bodies are two, but they are joined by a single head."

The *Bhagavad-gita* also describes the interconnectedness of pleasure and pain: "The non-permanent appearance of happiness and distress, and their disappearance in due course, are like the appearance and disappearance of winter and summer seasons. They arise of sense perception…

and one must learn to tolerate them without being disturbed."

Interestingly, recent psychological research has provided scientific evidence for the interconnectedness of pleasure and pain by showing that an experience that arouses one emotion in a person also seems to arouse its opposite. Called "affective contrast," it demonstrates that people appear to have an inbuilt "equilibrium regulator" that creates an aftereffect (in the opposing direction) for any experience that steers them away from a neutral emotional course. For example, any pleasurable experience is followed by a small, unpleasant aftereffect. If the pleasurable effect occurs again, the positive effect will remain constant, but the negative aftereffect will increase both in strength and duration. The pattern is acutely manifest in addictive behavior, where the initially powerful effect decreases until consumption becomes principally a means to ward off the negative "downside." One former drug abuser describes his addictive experience this way: "When I became 'strung out' on cocaine, the 'up' feeling I'd get from it would be less and less pleasurable, and the sensation would slip away more and more quickly. The 'downside ' would become so strong and enduring that I'd eventually feel like I was hooked up to an IV that was pumping pure anxiety into my body."

Addiction represents an extreme case that vividly illustrates the "roller-coaster" pattern, but as mentioned, affective contrast is not limited to addictive behavior. Research indicates that it accompanies nearly every feeling of pleasure achieved through sense (bodily) stimulation. Psychologist Barry Schwartz describes how people in general become caught up in this cycle of pleasure and disappointment: "People cannot derive pleasure from consuming the same old things. There is an inevitable disappointment that comes with consumption, because repeated consumption of the same commodities provides people with doses of pleasure that do not live up to their expectations – expectations shaped by their initial encounters with those commodities. As a result, people are driven to pursue novelty, to seek out new commodities whose pleasure potential has not yet been driven down by repeated consumption. But these new commodities will also fail to satisfy. The lesson is that the pursuit of pleasure is a wild goose chase. It requires people to be always on the lookout for new things. This may help explain the seemingly irrational and self-destructive thrill seeking that seems to characterize some especially affluent members of our affluent society."

This analysis supports the *sattvic* perspective that mental peace is the foundation of true happiness. Because real inner contentment is enduring, it is not achieved by accumulating more material acquisitions. As written by Lan Tao, "He who is content with what he has can never be despoiled. He who knows when to stop can never be destroyed." The *Upanishads* also advise people to be satisfied with their natural allotment. This is the principle of *tyaktena,* or being contented with our natural quota of enjoyment in our lives rather than letting our desires overwhelm us.

The principle of *tyaktena* does not proscribe that everyone must live a life of asceticism, only that we give up unnecessary striving for objects and experiences that we *imagine* will bring us completeness. It teaches that if we simply act righteously, in accord with our God-given natures, life's joys and sorrows will no longer be seen as objects to be passionately pursued or fearfully avoided. This higher perspective releases us from the tensions and anxieties induced by the modes of passion and ignorance, and brings about new insight into the true nature of happiness. As the Tao Te Ching states, "One who is filled with desire can see only the externals, while one free from desire can see the essence." There is also a beautiful *sloka* from the *Bhagavad-gita* in which Krishna tells Arjuna, "A person who is not disturbed by the incessant flow of desires – that enter like rivers into the ocean, which is ever being filled but is always still – can alone achieve peace, not the man who strives to satisfy such desires."

Chapter Six

Conclusion

Although thousands of years old, the spiritual principles encapsulated in *Eye of the Storm* are as relevant today as when originally recorded. As the sun, moon, and stars have lighted the world for every generation of mankind, so genuine spiritual wisdom illuminates our hearts irrespective of the world's changing social, cultural, or political conditions. Venerable spiritual literatures such as the *Bhagavad-gita* inform us that attachment, fear, and anger are the perpetual adversaries of the human mind, standing ever ready to disrupt our inherent serenity. But we also learn from these great teachings that by the grace of God it is possible to liberate our minds from these disquieting forces and directly experience the sustained and sublime pleasure of the transcendental realm.

As a final point, it should be stressed that while it is valuable to intellectually appreciate the ideas communicated in the classic writings of the East, deeper, more personal understanding requires applying them in our daily lives. The example is given in the *Vedas* that if we want to enjoy the sweetness of honey, we must move beyond admiring it through its glass jar and directly experience its taste.

Obviously, a broad discussion of how to practically integrate these principles would take us beyond the scope of this book, but the idea can be illustrated by briefly considering two examples. A first step in developing our natural humility is to appreciate God's friendship with all living entities. While the human form of life has the most highly developed intelligence of any species on this planet, other living beings also possess consciousness and feeling. To truly acknowledge their sentience requires that we show them basic respect and compassion, at least to the point of not inflicting unnecessary suffering upon them. Completely disregarding their interests in favor of our own enjoyment stems the development of humility and mercy. Specifically, any direct participation in the animal-killing industry (including purchasing and consuming flesh) will effectively prevent us from gaining the higher perspectives that invigorate real spiritual growth.

Practicing the spiritual science of meditation is a second example of how we can apply timeless Eastern principles in our modern lives. Admittedly, our turbulent times are not the most conducive to meditation, and as such, it may seem appropriate only for one who can retire to a mountaintop, tropical beach, or Himalayan cave. Interestingly, however, the nature of our modern era is anticipated and elaborately described in many ancient Eastern texts (it is generally referred to as *Kali Yuga*, or the Age of Quarrel and Hypocrisy). These writings explain that as a dispensation for the age we live in, the process of mantra meditation is especially powerful and easily performed. So in our stressful and hurried times, the rules of technique are largely relaxed in order to accommodate nearly any effort made by a practitioner.

The *bija*, or seed-sound, of any bona fide mantra is a Name of God, Who is the Original, Absolute Person. Filling our minds and senses with these divine sounds washes away the repositories of attachment, fear, and anger, just as rushing water carries off debris collected in a dry channel. Mantra meditation can be regularly performed while sitting or walking quietly, or even in moments of high anxiety or stress, in order to collect our emotions and connect with our inner selves.

As these examples show, the ancient spiritual writings of the East offer invaluable guidance in conducting our daily affairs, including how to run our offices, relate to family members, or even drive in traffic. Every day in every place, we experience the myriad energies of the world swirling about us, carrying our senses from one object to the next and pulling our minds from one idea to another. But as spiritual beings, we are of a different constitution than this world, and its changing nature need not disturb our core selves. This is the central lesson of the most profound teachings of the Eastern world. We sincerely hope that these immutable transcendental principles will enrich our readers' lives, as they have ours, and help point the way to the sublime pleasure of true spiritual realization.

References

1. *Bhagavad-gita As It Is* and *Srimad Bhagavatam*
His Divine Grace A.C. Bhaktivedanta Swami Prabhupada
Bhaktivedanta Book Trust (1973)

2. *Classical Indian Philosophy of Mind*
Kisor Kumar Chakrabarti
Albany: State University of New York Press (1999)

3. *Concept of Mind in Indian Philosophy*
Sarasvati Chennakesavan
Columbia, Mo.: South Indian Books (1980)

4. *Hindu Influence on Greek Philosophy*
Timothy Lomperis
Calcutta, India: Minerva

5. *Lao-Tzu and the Tao-te-ching*
Eds. Livia Kohn and Michael LaFarque
Albany, New York: SUNY Press

6. *The Sacred Books of China*
Translated by James Legge
Taipai: Ch'eng-Wen Publishing (1969)

7. *Creation's Journey: Native American Identity and Belief*
Eds. Tom Hill and Richard W. Hill, Sr.
Washington, D.C.: Smithsonian Institution Press(1997)

8. *Earth and Sky: Visions of the Cosmos in Native American Folklore*
Eds. Ray Williamson and Claire Farver
Albuquerque: Univ. of New Mexico Press (1992)

9. Manfred Stanley, "Beyond Progress" in *Images of the Future,* Ed. Robert Bundy
Buffalo: Prometheus Books (1976)

10. *Mind Over Matter: A Scientist's View of the Paranormal*
Kit Pedler
London: Thames Methuen (1987)

11. *A Philosophy of Matter and Mind*
Gerhard Wasserman
Aldershot, Hants, England: Avebury (1994)

12. *After Virtue*
Alistar MacIntyre
South Bend, Indiana: Univ. of Notre Dame Press(1981)

13. Gary Becker, E. Landis, and R. Michael
"An Economic Analysis of Marital Stability" in *Journal of Political Economy* 85 (1977)

14. *The Legitimation of Belief*
Ernest Gellner
Cambridge: Cambridge Univ. Press

15. *Beyond the Post-Modern Mind*
Huston Smith
Wheaton, Ill.: Theosophical Publishing House (1989)

16. *The Closing of the American Mind*
Allan Bloom
New York: Simon and Schuster (1987)

17. *Flow: The Psychology of Optimal Experience*
Mihaly Csikszentmihalyi
New York: Harper and Row (1990)

18. "*The City of Nine Gates*"
Michael Cremo
Paper presented at conference "Toward a Science of Consciousness" April 1996 at Univ. of Arizona

19. *The Battle for Human Nature*
Barry Schwartz
New York: W.W. Norton and CO. (1986)

BHAGAVAD-GITA AS IT IS

**By His Divine Grace
A.C. Bhaktivedanta
Swami Prabhupada**

The *Bhagavad-gita* is the concise summary of India's spiritual teachings. Remarkably, the setting for this classic is a battlefield. Just before the battle, the great warrior Arjuna begins to inquire from Lord Krishna about the meaning of life. The *Gita* systematically guides one along the path of self-realization. It is the main source book for information on karma, reincarnation, yoga, devotion, the soul, Lord Krishna, and spiritual enlightenment. *Bhagavad-gita As It Is* is the best-selling edition in the world!

> "*Bhagavad-gita As It Is* is a deeply felt, powerfully conceived, and beautifully explained work. I have never seen any other work on the *Gita* with such an important voice and style. It is a work of undoubted integrity. It will occupy a significant place in the intellectual and ethical life of modern man for a long time to come." —Dr. Shaligram Shukla, Assistant Professor of Linguistics, Georgetown University

**Deluxe edition with translations and elaborate purports:
$24.95 ♦ ISBN 0-89213-285-X ♦ 6.5" x 9.5"
♦ Hardbound ♦ 1068 pgs. ♦ 29 full-color plates
Standard edition, including translations and elaborate purports:
$12.95 ♦ ISBN 0-89213-123-3 ♦ 5.5" x 8.5"
♦ Hardbound ♦ 924 pgs. ♦ 14 full-color plates**

INTERACTIVE BHAGAVAD-GITA AS IT IS ON CD!

**For Mac or PC CD- Rom, over 30 hours of Audio, 275 full-color illustrations, video clips, and nearly 1,000 pages of text.
$19.95 ISBN 91-7149-415-4**

BHAGAVAD-GITA
THE SONG DIVINE

A New, Easy-to-Understand Edition of India's Timeless Masterpiece of Spiritual Wisdom

The *Bhagavad-gita*, India's greatest spiritual treatise, contains far too much drama to remain the exclusive property of philosophers and religionists. Woodham presents the timeless wisdom of the *Gita* in contemporary English poetry, bringing to life its ancient yet perennially applicable message. It recounts in metered stanzas the historic conversation between Krishna, the Supreme Mystic, and the mighty warrior Arjuna as they survey the battlefield preparations for the greatest world war of all time. This reader-friendly edition will attract the minds and hearts of not only spiritualists and philosophers, but of dramatists, musicians, children, poetry-lovers, and all who seek inspiration in their daily lives.

$15.00 ♦ ISBN 1-887089-26-8
♦ 5" x 7" ♦ Hardcover ♦ 118 pgs.

Book Order Form

- Telephone orders: Call 1-888-TORCHLT (1-888-867-2458)
  (Please have your credit card ready.)
- Fax orders: 559-337-2354
- Postal Orders: Torchlight Publishing, 49334 Stagecoach Drive, Badger, CA 93603, USA www.torchlight.com

Please send the following:	Quantity	Amount
❒ **Bhagavad-gita As It Is**		
Deluxe (1,068 pages)—$24.95	x______	= $______
Standard (924 pages)—$12.95	x______	= $______
❒ **Bhagavad-gita Interactive CD**—$19.95	x______	= $______
❒ **Bhagavad-gita The Song Divine**—$15.00	x______	= $______

Shipping/handling (see below)________________ $______
Sales tax 7.25% (California only)________________ $______
TOTAL ________________ $______

(I understand that I may return any book for a full refund—no questions asked.)

❒ Please send your catalog and info on other books by Torchlight Publishing

Company ________________________________

Name ________________________________

Address ________________________________

City ____________________ State ______ Zip ______

Payment:

❒ Check/money order enclosed ❒ VISA ❒ MasterCard ❒ American Express

Card number ________________________________

Name on card ____________________ Exp. date ______

Signature ________________________________

Shipping and handling:

USA: $4.00 for the first book and $3.00 for each additional book.
Airmail per book (USA only)—$7.00.
Canada: $6.00 for the first book and $3.50 for each additional book.
(NOTE: Please allow 3 to 4 weeks for delivery in North America.)
Foreign countries: $8.00 for the first book and $5.00 for each additional book. Please allow 6 to 8 weeks for delivery.